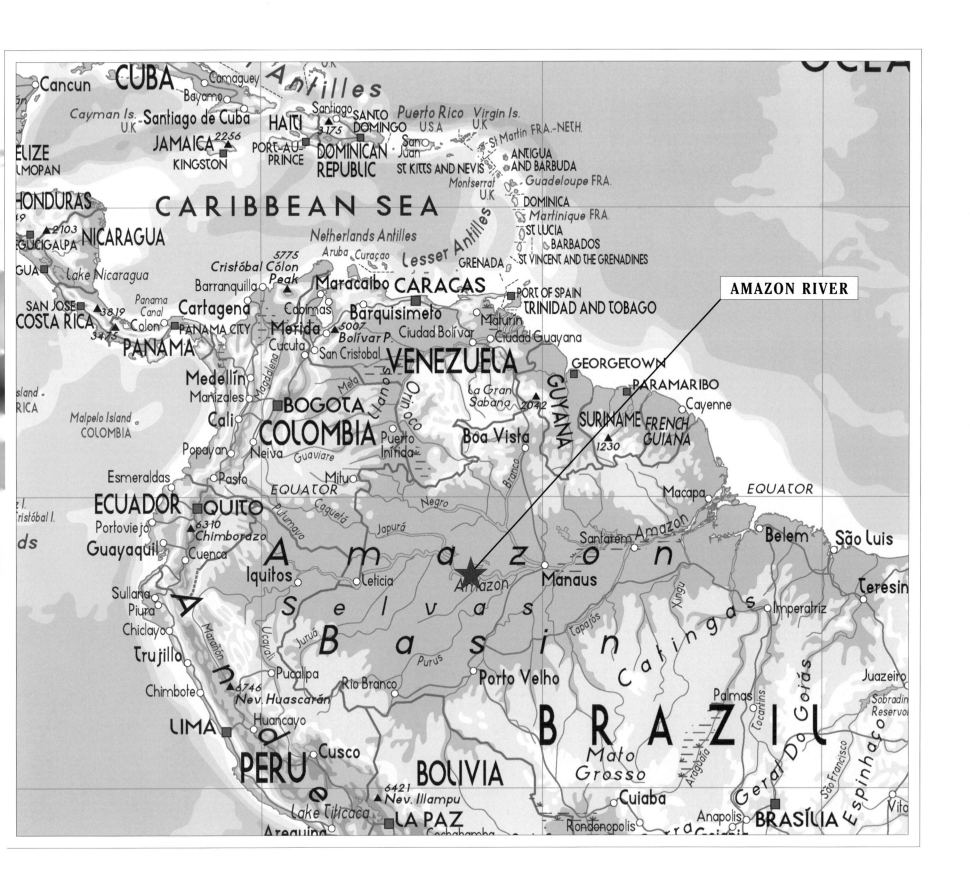

#53306346

1-31-06

Published by Creative Education
123 South Broad Street
Mankato, Minnesota 56001

Creative Education is an imprint of The Creative Company.

Designed by Stephanie Blumenthal
Production design by The Design Lab

Photographs by Jay Ireland and Georgienne Bradley/Bradley Ireland Productions, Betty Crowell, Corbis (Ricardo
Azoury, Bettmann, Tom Brakefield, COLLART HERVE/CORBIS SYGMA, CORBIS SYGMA, Michael Freeman,
Paulo Fridman, Gustavo Gilabert/CORBIS SABA, Dave G. Houser, Hulton-Deutsch Collection, Wolfgang Kaehler,
Layne Kennedy, Danny Lehman, Richard List, Craig Lovell, Buddy Mays, Joe McDonald, Digital image © 1996
CORBIS; Original image courtesy of NASA, Reuters, Galen Rowell, Royalty-Free, Kevin Schafer, Swim Ink, Nik
Wheeler, Staffan Widstrand, Alison Wright, Jim Zuckerman), Geoatlas/World Vector 3 Map CD, James P. Rowan

Printed in the United States of America

Library of Congress Cataloging-in-Publication Data

Fitzpatrick, Anne, 1978–
Amazon River / by Anne Fitzpatrick.
p. cm. — (Natural wonders of the world)
Summary: An overview of South America's Amazon River, which is approximately 4,000 miles long.
ISBN 1-58341-322-7
1. Amazon River—Juvenile literature. [1. Amazon River.] I. Title. II. Series.

F2546.F56 2004   918.1'1—dc22   2003062574

First edition

2 4 6 8 9 7 5 3 1

AMAZON RIVER

THE MIGHTY RIVER-SEA

The Amazon River falls 16,400 feet (5,000 m) in its first 600 miles (970 km) through the Andes. There are no waterfalls on the Amazon outside of the Andes. The river's current averages 1.5 miles (2.5 km) per hour during the dry season and 3 miles (5 km) per hour during the rainy season.

After leaving its humble roots in the Andes mountains (right), the Amazon River winds its way past thousands of miles of isolated forest and the occasional village or city.

The Yagua Indians of Peru tell of a great storm long ago, when wind and thunder shook the earth. In the midst of the storm, a giant tree fell. Its trunk sank deep into the earth and became a huge torrent of water that rushed toward the sea. The tree's branches became smaller rivers. Leaves became fish, and pieces of the trunk became large canoes filled with the Yagua and other peoples. This was, they said, the birth of the Amazon, a river system so vast that early Portuguese explorers called it *O Rio Mar*, meaning "The River-Sea."

From the air, it is easy to see why the Yagua compared the Amazon River and its **tributaries** to a tree. The sprawling network

of rivers spreads across most of the northern half of South America. Smaller rivers join larger rivers, which add their currents to the great Amazon River itself. Twenty percent of the Earth's freshwater is carried by the Amazon River and its tributaries. Some sections of the Amazon River are so wide that a person on a boat in the center of the river cannot see the banks on either side.

The farthest **headwaters** of the Amazon River are 17,200 feet (5,240 m) above **sea level**, in the Andes mountains of Peru, where a small stream called the Apurímac River issues from the rocks and flows northwest to join the Ucayali River. The Ucayali flows north through the Andes, then turns east to

The Amazon River carries more water than any other river in the world—more than the Mississippi, Nile, and Yangtze combined. It dumps an average of 57 million gallons (214 million l) per second into the ocean. In just two hours, it dumps enough water to supply New York City for a year.

So mighty that not a single bridge crosses it at any point, the Amazon River branches out into more than 1,000 tributaries—17 of which are more than 1,000 miles (1,600 km) long.

meet the Marañón River near Iquitos, Peru. Together they become the Amazon River, flowing east across Brazil to the Atlantic Ocean. It is impossible to give an exact length of the river because river channels constantly change, but from **source** to **mouth**, through all its curves, the Amazon River is about 4,000 miles (6,400 km) long.

The Amazon river system drains 38 percent of South America, an area roughly the size of Australia. Because peak rainfall is received at different times of the year in different parts of the Amazon's course, it is only during October and November that the river is typically not flooded anywhere along its length. There may be 30 feet (9 m) difference between the high and low water levels of the

river. The **floodplain** extends an average of 30 miles (48 km)—and in some places up to 180 miles (300 km)—on each side of the river, creating the unique flooded forests of the Amazon.

One hundred and forty million years ago, the ancestor of the mighty Amazon drained a much larger continent. South America, India, and Africa were one large mass of land. The river flowed east to west, draining into the Pacific Ocean. After South America separated and began to drift west, the formation of the Andes mountains between 25 and 50 million years ago blocked the western flow of the river, causing it to reverse its course and flow backwards into the Atlantic, as the Amazon continues to do today.

RIVER OF LIFE

The blue face, red eyes, and red, feathered crest of a bird called the hoatzin make it one of the Amazon rain forest's most striking creatures. When alarmed, the hoatzin will dive into water. It has claws on the ends of its wings, which it uses to climb back to its nest when its feathers are too wet to fly.

The warm, wet climate of the Amazon region supports a huge variety of life. More than one-third of all the plant and animal species in the world live in the Amazon River **basin**. The river system is home to more species of freshwater fish than any other part of the world. Scientists have found more than 3,000 plant species in just one square mile (2.6 sq km) of the rain forest that covers the Amazon basin. Half of the world's species of birds live along the river or in the surrounding jungle.

One of the Amazon's most infamous residents is the piranha, a flat, oval-shaped fish with razor-sharp teeth. Despite the fish's fearsome reputation, attacks on humans and large mammals are rare. Another unique fish, called the tambaqui, lives on the fruit and seeds that fall into the water of the flooded forests, fasting during low water periods. The piramutaba catfish is believed to migrate about 2,050 miles (3,300 km) from the mouth of the Amazon River to its spawning grounds in the foothills of the Andes mountains.

The pink river dolphin swims gracefully between the tree trunks of the flooded forest despite its seven-foot (2 m) length. One local legend says that the dolphins take on human form to dance with the women of the villages on the banks of the river, wearing hats to hide their blowholes. Other river mammals include the manatee and the giant river otter. The giant otter grows up to six feet (1.8 m)

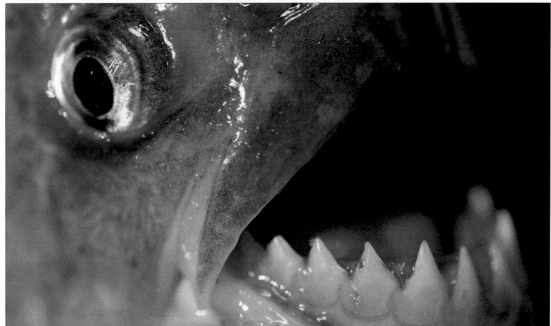

The Amazon River basin includes a stunning variety of creatures. The Amazonian manatee (opposite bottom) swims along the river bottom, while the colorful hoatzin (opposite top) nests in branches overhanging the river. The sharp-toothed piranha (bottom left and top left) is a fearsome predator that competes with egrets (below) for prey.

The red uakari is a monkey with a bald, bright red face and shaggy fur, found only in the Amazon rain forest. Measuring about 22 inches (55 cm) and weighing about 8 pounds (4 kg), the red uakari can leap up to 80 feet (25 m) from tree to tree.

The golden lion tamarin (right) is among the most endangered mammals in the world. It is one of nature's great acrobats, able to leap incredible distances between trees in the forest canopy.

long and can weigh 70 pounds (32 kg). Its valuable fur has made it the most endangered animal in the Amazon region.

The anaconda, the world's largest snake at up to 30 feet (9 m) and 200 pounds (90 kg), floats in the river with its eyes just above the surface, awaiting its prey. It might get lucky when a heron or egret dives for fish, but it must compete with the **endangered** black caiman, a 20-foot (6 m) crocodile, for food.

Plant life is plentiful throughout the river, especially in the still waters of the flooded forests. Colonies of giant Amazon water lilies float on the surface; their leaves may be as long as seven feet (2 m). Floating meadows, created when cane grass and other rooted plants growing in shallow water are uprooted by rising water levels, drift downriver. Much of the Amazon floodplain is heavily forested. Palm trees and Brazil nut trees are plentiful. The beautiful giant of the rain forest, the kapok tree, can grow up to 150 feet (46 m) tall. Near the coast, the river is bordered by swampy mangrove forests.

In the rain forest canopy, monkeys screech and scamper, and toucans, macaws, and parrots perch, staying high and dry even during the floods. Some land animals adapt easily to the yearly influx of water; the jaguar, a large, spotted cat, and the capybara, the world's largest rodent, are both strong swimmers. Iguanas dive into the water when frightened and can stay on the bottom for hours by holding their breath.

The region surrounding the Amazon River features a great diversity of habitats. In places, there is little separation between Brazilian beaches, densely wooded rain forest, and lily-filled lagoons. One of the kings of the rain forest is the jaguar (below), a powerful cat that can weigh up to 300 pounds (136 kg).

The Amazon rain forest
is more densely packed
with animal life than
any other environment
on Earth. The forest
canopy provides dry
roosting for many bird
species, including dozens
of types of parrot (right).
Although it will venture
into trees as well, the
anaconda (below) is
more at home on the
ground or in the water.

Famous for its painfully slow movements, the sloth (left) would be easy prey for many predators if it did not live so high off the ground. The green iguana (below) climbs easily through the forest canopy and is a strong swimmer as well. To escape danger, it has been known to drop to the ground from great heights and dive into water.

TAMING THE AMAZON

Humans have long dwelled in the Amazon rain forest. Many native peoples today live the same primitive lifestyle of their ancestors, hunting with poison darts and fashioning basic tools. Dugout canoes, carved from great logs, continue to be used on the river and its tributaries.

The earliest known human habitation in the Amazon River basin is evidenced by a site containing the remains of stone tools, a fire ring, and butchered bird bone that scientists date to about 12,000 years ago. Before the arrival of Europeans, the people of the Amazon lived in small, **nomadic** groups, hunting with poison-tipped arrows and blow guns and traveling the river in dugout canoes.

In about 1500, Spanish explorer Vincente Pinzón entered the Amazon River from the coast, sailing partway up the lower river in search of gold. In 1541 and 1542, another Spaniard, Francisco de Orellana, explored from the mouth of the Napo River in Peru all the way to the mouth of the Amazon in the Atlantic, a journey of 1,875 miles (3,017 km). At one point on their journey, he and his party were attacked by female warriors with bows and arrows. Orellana called them Amazons, after the female warriors of Greek mythology, and the name was later given to the river itself.

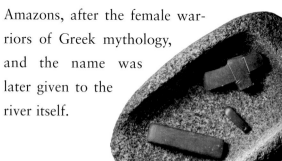

18

Englishman Alfred Russel Wallace lived in the Amazon rain forest from 1848 to 1852 developing his theory of "survival of the fittest." He later shared his conclusions with English scientist Charles Darwin, who was then working on his famous book, *On the Origin of Species.*

In the mid-1800s, the Amazon region experienced a rubber boom. North Americans and Europeans took over large parts of the rain forest to tap rubber trees, sending the raw liquid downriver by boat. Many Indians were killed or enslaved during this period. Steamships appeared on the Amazon in the 1860s to carry rubber and other raw materials from the jungle to the coast, and many trees were cut down for firewood to power the ships. By 1913, British rubber production in Malaysia had taken off, and the South American rubber trade all but disappeared.

Today the people who live on the Amazon River are largely *mestizo*, a mixture of Spanish and Indian. Most live in open-sided houses on stilts with thatched palm roofs. There are three major port cities, each with more than one million people. Iquitos is about 2,300 miles (3,700 km) up the Amazon River from the Atlantic, in Peru. Manaus, Brazil, the largest of the three, is about 1,000 miles (1,600 km) from the mouth of the Amazon. Belém, Brazil, is on the Pará River, about 90 miles (145 km) from the Atlantic coast. Animal skins, Brazil nuts, lumber, rubber, and live birds, fish, and animals are transported on the river for export. Cattle ranching and fishing are the primary industries in the Amazon River basin today.

Over the years, the Amazon rain forest has provided fascinating study subjects for scientists such as Alfred Russel Wallace (opposite top), simple home-building materials for local peoples, land for farming, and—increasingly—lumber for the logging industry.

The Yanomami Indians
of the Amazon River
basin may be the last cul-
ture to have come into
contact with the modern
world. They continue to
live in relative isolation
deep in the rain forest,
hunting with poison
darts shot by bows and
blow guns, fishing, and
tending small gardens.

Approximately 20,000 Yanomami Indians live in the northern part of the Amazon rain forest today. This isolated tribe, which had virtually no contact with the outside world before the 1980s, has spurned modern technology and continues to rely completely on the jungle's natural resources for its survival.

THE AMAZON AT RISK

Scientists call the Amazon a whitewater river, which means it is muddy with **sediment**. Blackwater rivers have little sediment and a sandy riverbed; clearwater rivers have little sediment and a clay riverbed. When blackwater or clearwater rivers flow into the Amazon River, they create striking contrasts as the waters meet.

The tributaries of the Amazon River provide an array of water coloration, fish for market, and energy in the form of hydroelectric dams.

A total of about 150,000 to 200,000 tons (136,000–181,500 t) of fish are harvested in the Amazon River basin each year, but the populations of fewer than five species have been seriously affected. Cattle ranching has been much more damaging. Ranchers clear land in the Amazon basin in order to graze cattle and water buffalo. Any plants and trees that have not been cleared are trampled by the animals. Damage to vegetation affects the fish and wildlife that feed on it, which affects the wildlife that feed on them, setting off a terrible chain reaction.

The paths that the animals tread through the vegetation eventually become channels of water, draining the floodplains more quickly than would occur naturally. The hot sun,

in the absence of shade from trees that were cleared, also causes waterways to dry up more quickly and more extensively. The destruction of floodplain streams can be very damaging to fish and aquatic animals.

Pesticides from farming and pollution from cities have had some effect on the river as well. One of the greatest threats to the Amazon region, however, is from **hydroelectric** dams. Although damming the Amazon River itself has never been seriously considered, there are dams on many tributaries, and many more are proposed. Dams are very disruptive to fish populations, particularly migratory fish, which may find the path of their annual migration blocked. The forest upriver from the dam becomes permanently submerged. The river

The pirarucu is one of the largest fish in the Amazon river system. It grows up to 10 feet (3 m) long and averages 200 pounds (90 kg). It has dark green scales that turn crimson toward the tail. The pirarucu breathes air, staying underwater for only 10 to 20 minutes at a time.

The pirarucu (right) is a huge fish known for its armor-like scales. Its range includes the protected Negro River in Brazil—a part of which is shown here (opposite) in a photograph taken from space.

below the dam often becomes smaller and slower, and land downriver receives fewer nutrients because of the reduced water flow and filtering by the dam.

Although there are several areas along the river that are designated for **conservation** by the Brazilian government, including the entire **estuary** region, there is no active conservation and enforcement being carried out in them. The only land along the Amazon River that is protected is that at the meeting of the Amazon and the Japura rivers: the Mamirauá Sustainable Development Reserve is an area covering more than 4,250 square miles (11,000 sq km), one-third of which is protected from development. It is an experiment in conservation in which people are permitted to live within the reserve,

and the residents help to make decisions about conservation and development.

It is estimated that 7,800 square miles (20,200 sq km) of Amazon rain forest are destroyed each year—an area the size of New Jersey. Experts believe that more than 200,000 square miles (518,000 sq km) of rain forest have already been destroyed—an area approximately equal to the area of France. The fragile environment of the Amazon River basin is under siege, and the lives of many rare and beautiful creatures hang in the balance. It is only with committed effort and thoughtful management that the mighty Amazon River and the incomparable habitat it supports will continue to fill future generations with wonder.

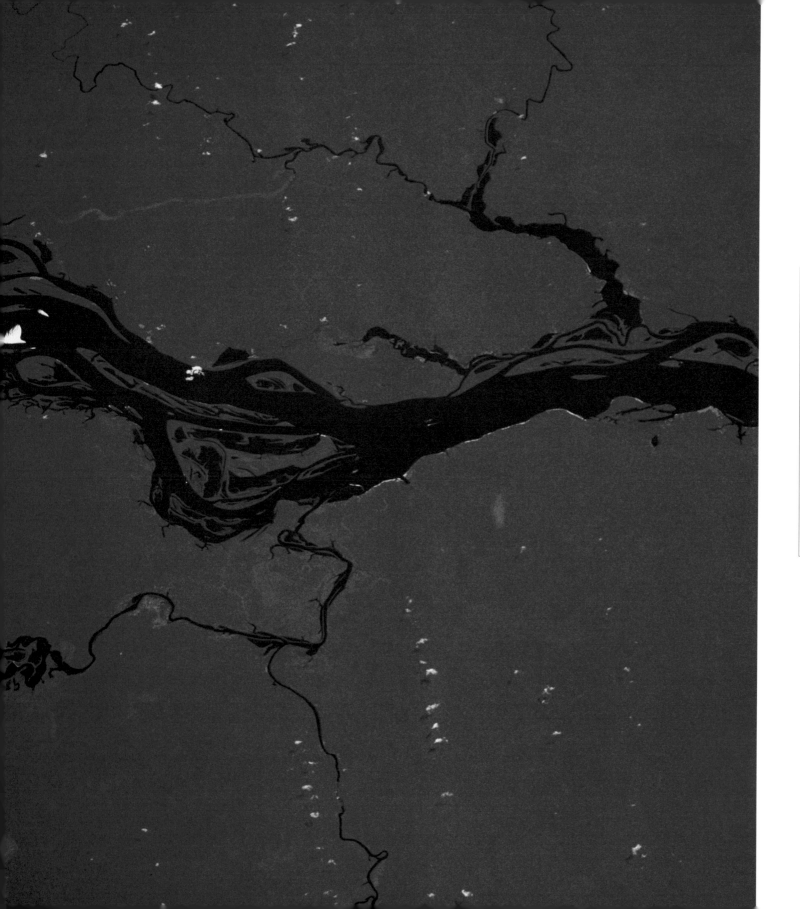

The Central Amazon
Conservation Complex,
including Jaú National
Park, was created in
1980 and expanded in
recent years. It is the
largest protected area in
the Amazon River basin,
covering 8,800 square
miles (22,700 sq km)
along the lower Negro
River in Brazil.

SEEING THE WONDER

Many visitors to the Amazon region come for the exotic wildlife. Among the best ways to see the sights is from boats traveling the river and tributaries near such popular destinations as Manaus, Brazil. Crocodiles (below) are commonly seen on riverbanks and are the featured attraction at the Crocodile Safari Zoo near Belém, Brazil.

The best way to explore the Amazon River is, of course, by boat. Options vary from Brazil's luxurious, state-run yachts with air-conditioned cabins, live music, pools, and restaurants, to cargo-carrying riverboats, on which most passengers sleep on hammocks on deck. Tour boats are more comfortable than most riverboats, travel closer to the riverbank, and have open upper decks for better views. The 993-mile (1,602 km) trip from Belém to Manaus takes about three to five days.

Belém is a large river port founded in 1616 by the Portuguese. Colorful colonial

buildings, mansions dating to the early 20th-century rubber boom, and modern high-rises create a fascinating architectural mix. There is a variety of hotels in Belém, from the comfortable Hilton International to the cozy, inexpensive Manacá Hotel. Fishing trips can be arranged, and the Crocodile Safari Zoo, a research station with more than 500 crocodiles, is a short trip through the rain forest by jeep.

Manaus is popular because of its many nearby jungle lodges. The Amazon Lodge offers floating cabins, and the Ariaú Jungle Tower lodge consists of four wooden towers

Although much of the Amazon region remains untamed, the great river is not untouched by the modern world. It carries great cruise ships, is overlooked by historic mansions in such cities as Belém, Brazil (bottom left), and has given birth to sprawling port cities such as Iquitos, Peru (bottom right).

The Amazon River and its surrounding rain forest truly are a natural wonder. Counting the river's many tributaries, the region includes more than 11,000 miles (17,600 km) of waterway, hundreds of ports both big and small, and sights that can be found nowhere else in the world.

connected by catwalks. Half- or full-day boat trips from Manaus include excursions to the meeting of the Negro's black waters with the yellow-brown waters of the Amazon. At night, Manaus offers the Boi-Bumbá, a presentation of live music, storytelling, and dancing by men and women in Indian costumes.

Seeing the Amazon River requires crossing international borders. You will need a **passport** to enter Colombia and Peru, and Brazil requires a **visa**. Once in the country, you must exchange money for the local currency. Brazil's currency is the *real*; Columbia uses the *peso*; and Peru, the *nuevo sol*. Language will be another barrier; most people in the Amazon basin speak Portuguese, Spanish, or one of many Indian languages, and people outside of major cities speak little or no English.

Sunscreen and insect repellent are essential items for any trip to the rain forest. Throughout the Amazon River basin, be sure to drink only bottled water, and wash and peel fruit before eating it, to avoid getting sick. Before leaving home, you should get vaccinations for diseases such as hepatitis A and typhoid, which are spread by infected food and water, and yellow fever, which is spread by mosquitoes.

A M A Z O N   R I V E R

QUICK FACTS

Location: Northern South America, through parts of Brazil, Colombia, and Peru

Source: In the province of Cailloma, Peru, in the Andes mountains

Mouth: Northeastern Brazil

Length: 3,950–4,200 miles (6,400–6,800 km)

Average width: 1.5 to 6 miles (2.4–10 km)

Widest point: 90 miles (140 km) at the mouth

Average depth: 40 feet (12 m)

Deepest point: 300 feet (90 m)

Age: More than 140 million years

Early explorers: Spanish explorers Vincente Pinzón (1500) and Francisco de Orellana (1541–42)

Protected areas: Mamirauá Sustainable Development Reserve in Brazil, established in 1992

Average temperature (year-round): 80 °F (27 °C)

Annual rainfall: 50 to 120 inches (130–300 cm)

Wildlife: Includes piranha, tambaqui, catfish, dolphins, giant river otters, manatees, anacondas, boa constrictors, black caiman, giant river turtles, tree frogs, monkeys, jaguars, capybaras, sloths, herons, egrets, toucans, macaws, parrots, bats, tarantulas, butterflies, ants

Other names: *Amazonas*, *Ucayali* (Peru), *Solimões* (Brazil)

GLOSSARY

basin—all the land drained by a river and its tributaries

conservation—the protection and management of natural resources, such as forests, rivers, and wildlife

endangered—a species of animal or plant that is at risk of becoming extinct (dying out completely); threatened species are at risk of becoming endangered

estuary—the lower part or wide mouth of a river where the saltwater tide meets the fresh-water current

floodplain—relatively flat land bordering a stream, lake, or river that is subject to flooding

headwaters—the streams in which a river originates

hydroelectric—producing electricity by water power, such as by harnessing the flow of a river

mouth—the part of a river where the water empties into another body of water

nomadic—having no permanent home; instead, moving around in search of food, pasture, or other resources

passport—a document issued by a country to one of its citizens, allowing that person to travel to other countries and re-enter his or her home country

sea level—the level of the surface of the sea, used as a standard in measuring heights and depths

sediment—small pieces of matter, such as soil, rocks, or dead plants, deposited by water or wind

source—a spring, lake, or other body of water that is the starting point for a stream or river

tributaries—streams or rivers that flow into a larger stream or river

visa—stamp on a passport giving someone permission to enter or pass through a country; some countries require that a visa be obtained before entering

INDEX